A BEAR-BRAINED ADVENTURE

WRITTEN BY
CHARIS MATHER

BookLife freedom Readers

BookLife
PUBLISHING

©2023 BOOKLIFE PUBLISHING LTD.
KING'S LYNN, NORFOLK, PE30 4LS, UK

ISBN 978-1-80505-047-6

A BEAR-BRAINED ADVENTURE

WRITTEN BY CHARIS MATHER
BASED ON A STORY BY ROBIN TWIDDY
EDITED BY KIRSTY HOLMES
ILLUSTRATED BY WANQING WU

ABOUT THE AUTHORS

AS A YOUNG GIRL, CHARIS' BEDTIME STORIES WERE MADE UP OF 50% EPIC ADVENTURES AND 50% DRAMATIC COPYRIGHT FRONT MATTER READINGS. WHILE CHARIS HAS HER SUSPICIONS ABOUT THE ORIGINS OF HER INSPIRATION TO WORK WITH BOOKS, SHE HAS NEVER QUITE BEEN ABLE TO PUT HER FINGER ON IT. A PROFESSIONAL WRITER AT WORK AND A PROFESSIONAL DAYDREAMER AT HOME, CHARIS SPENDS A LOT OF TIME SPINNING STORIES IN HER HEAD... SOME OF WHICH HAVE EVEN MADE IT ONTO PAPER!

ROBIN HAS ALWAYS LOVED STORIES. AS A CHILD, HE WOULD OFTEN BE FOUND DAYDREAMING, LOST IN YET ANOTHER TALE IN HIS HEAD. AS AN ADULT, HE HAS HAD THE GREAT PRIVILEGE OF TAKING THOSE STORIES IN HIS HEAD AND SHARING THEM WITH CHILDREN ALL AROUND THE WORLD. ROBIN LIVES WITH HIS PARTNER AND THEIR TWO YOUNG GIRLS, WHO HAVE PROVEN TO BE A WELLSPRING OF JOY AND INSPIRATION FOR HIM.

ABOUT THE ILLUSTRATOR

WANQING BEGAN DRAWING AT A YOUNG AGE AND NEVER STOPPED. IN THE YEARS THAT FOLLOWED, SHE SPENT TIME WORKING AS A JOURNALIST. THIS EXPERIENCE PROVIDED HER WITH AN OBSERVANT EYE FOR DETAIL AND A THOUGHTFUL APPROACH TO HER SUBJECTS. SHE CARRIED THESE GIFTS OVER TO HER ILLUSTRATION WORK. IT IS THROUGH HER ART THAT SHE EXPRESSES THIS OBSERVANT NATURE AND HER WONDERFUL SENSE OF HUMOUR. HER LOVE FOR NATURE AND WILDLIFE ALMOST LED HER TO BECOMING A WILDLIFE CONSERVATIONIST. HOWEVER, NOW, WANQING WORKS AS A FREELANCE ILLUSTRATOR IN LONDON.

CHAPTER 1

IAN THE BARBARIAN

Across the wild lands of Fabiosa, no name was feared quite as much as that of Ian the Barbarian. A living legend in a world of dragons, goblins and door-to-door salesmen, Ian was known across the land.

Some said that Ian's fearsomeness came from his powerful build. Some said it was because of his huge brain. Some even said it was all thanks to his intimidating haircut (although, anyone who had ever met Ian in person might have disagreed).

There was one thing about Ian the Barbarian that no one disagreed on. If Ian set his mind on something, there was nothing that could stop him. No one could out-barbarian Ian.

Tonight, Ian's mind was set on a mysterious glowing orb. Ian didn't know whose orb it was, nor what it did, but he did know that it was shiny. And if Ian knew anything, it was that shiny things were worth a lot of gold. Ian liked gold.

Ian thought back to the first time he had heard of the Orb of Animatia...

Back before he had bashed in the back

door of this twisted tower and bounded
up its bajillion steps...

Back before he had waded through
the Smelly Swamps and defeated that
band of shapeshifting goblins...

Back all the way to a simple card game at the Fabled Inn.

Ian remembered the game well. He had played against a small, rat-faced man in a hood. The hooded man had been crafty enough, but he was no match for Ian's barbarian brain. Of course, Ian had won completely fairly. Anyone who had been there would tell you that the barbarian's huge size and strength and threatening grunting had absolutely nothing to do with Ian's win. In fact, Ian

won so completely
fairly that the
hooded man even
shared a juicy
secret with him
as a prize. The
man told Ian exactly
where to find an orb worth a thousand
gold pieces!

And now, after a trek that had taken
the barbarian halfway across Fabiosa,
here it was in front of him. The orb
sat right in the middle of the tower's
uppermost room, easier to snatch than a
rattle from a baby.

The hooded man hadn't lied (of course he hadn't – why would he lie after such a fair, friendly game?). All Ian had to do was reach out and grab the orb...

CHAPTER 2

THE TRANSFORMATION

Ian wasn't sure what he had expected to happen when the orb was finally in his hands, but it certainly wasn't for his fingers and elbows to go numb. He hadn't expected weird, glowing lights to come out of it and wrap around him, either.

"Eh?" Ian said to himself, confused. Ian felt weird.

Maybe he was just hungry... or tired? It was probably nothing. Ian was sure that the strange feeling would go away in just a minute, but he put the orb down just in case. There must be something else shiny he could swipe from this strange room full of weird flasks and old books...

Ian looked around. In the corner of the room there was a large mirror, and looking right at him from inside it was a huge bear! He jumped in surprise.

So did the bear.

Hang on.

A bear inside a mirror?

Did that mean…?

"I… I'M A BEAR?"
roared Ian. He stumbled
backwards, tripping over
his own large, furry paws.
Ian landed on his backside
with a thump.

"Shouldn't have touched the orb…"
squawked a voice from the shadows
above. Ian heard a soft flutter, which
was quickly followed by a flash of green

feathers. Down from the tower rafters swooped a parrot with a wonky wizard's hat atop its head. The bird had a pair of smart spectacles on, through which it was peering at Ian. "I should know. It's my orb."

"Who are you?" Ian growled through his new teeth.

"My name is Waypine," replied the parrot. "I wasn't always a parrot, you know.

I was once a powerful wizard. A clumsy, orb-touching wizard."

Ian would probably have been more surprised by the talking wizard parrot if he hadn't just been magically turned into a bear.

"I've got bad news for you, I'm afraid," Waypine said, pushing his spectacles up his beak with one wing. "You and I have both been cursed by that bothersome Orb of Animatia."

"I'll smash it!" Ian said, jumping up.

"Oh, no, no, no," Waypine

interrupted quickly. "We can't smash it. We'd be stuck in these bodies forever. There is only one thing in all of Fabiosa that can undo the curse... the Crown of Humanagain. There's just one teensy problem, though."

"What?" snarled the bear.

"The crown has been split into four pieces and spread out across the land," said Waypine as he flapped onto Ian's shoulder. "Thankfully, I know where each piece is. Come now – we've got quite the journey ahead of us!"

CHAPTER 3

THE GIANT GIANT

And just like that, the two most unlikely adventuring partners in Fabiosa set off together to find the pieces of a magical crown. Ian and his new wizard companion journeyed through swamp and field, over hill and valley.

"If you know so much about this crown, why haven't you collected the pieces yourself?" Ian asked as he walked.

"Oh, you'll see…" said Waypine. "Why don't you take a look for yourself, just over this hill."

Ian strode up to the very top of the hill to see what the wizard was so worried about. There, lying down at the bottom of the valley, was a huge, sleeping giant.

"Huh," said Ian.

Ian spotted a glint of light by the giant's ear. A shiny, green jewel hung from a gold earring.

"There!" said Waypine. "You see it? That's the first part of the crown."

"No problem," Ian growled. "Stay here." Ian had his eyes on the prize. The bear reached for his dagger and charged straight for the giant and his earring. "Prepare to die..."

Before Ian had made it two steps, the dagger had slipped from his paws.

"You don't have any thumbs. You can't hold a dagger." Waypine pointed out to his companion. "And now you've woken the giant up!"

Ian gave up on the dagger. He didn't need it anyway. Why bother with that tiny thing when he could use his new claws instead? He charged again. Waypine watched from the sky as the giant reached out and flicked the tiny bear away with his massive fingers.

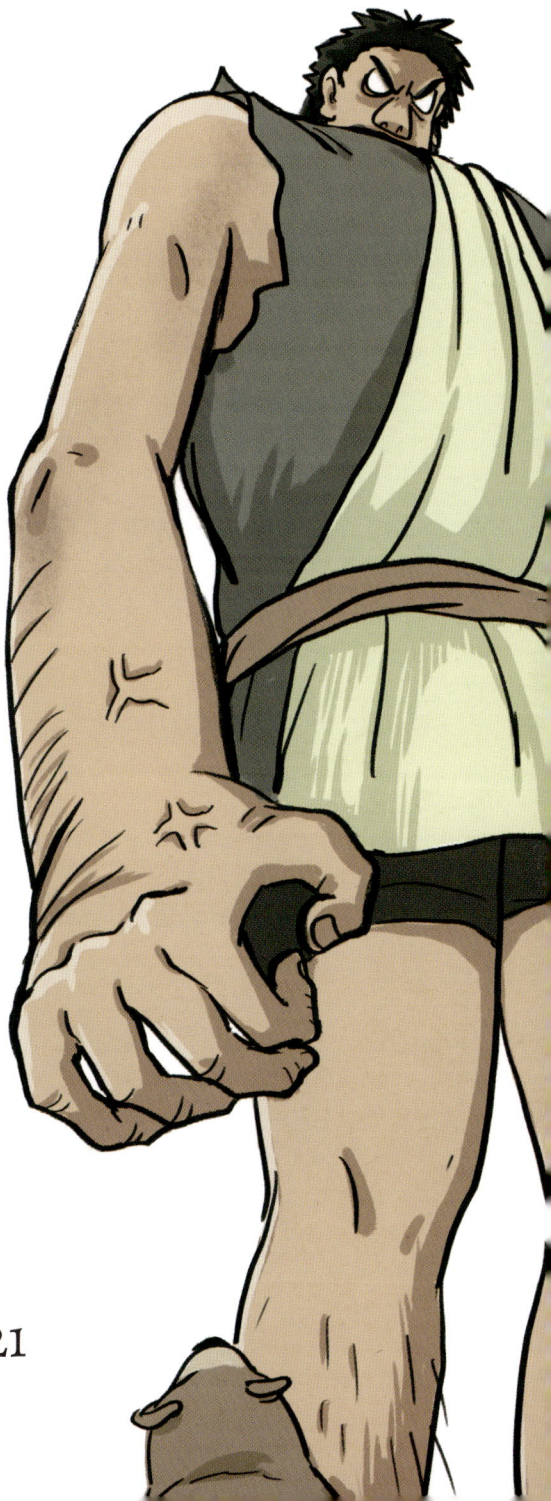

Ian
went sailing
over the next hill.

"Oh dear," said the
wizard.

Anyone else would have
given up at that point. But Ian was no
ordinary adventurer. He barrelled straight
back to the giant, leapt onto its hairy leg–

–and was flicked straight off again.

And again.

And again.

And again.

Waypine watched the bear climb and fall, climb and fall, climb and fall. "I think he might be too stupid to die," he marvelled to himself.

Eventually, the giant had had enough. He reached down and plucked the little bear up by the scruff of his neck.

"ENOUGH!" yelled the giant. "WHAT YOU WANT, LITTLE BEAR?"

"The earring!" Ian roared back. The giant looked confused.

"I don't believe he
understands bear,"
said Waypine. "Let
me translate... He
said he would like your
earring."

"Fine, take it. Just leave
me alone," the giant grumbled. He
took out the earring and flicked the tiny
jewel at the bird and the bear. As Ian and
Waypine admired their prize, the grumpy
giant lumbered off to look for a new spot
to nap where he wouldn't be interrupted
by any more annoying adventurers.

Much to Waypine's surprise, the first part of the quest had been a success. Ian was not surprised at all. He tucked the jewel away in his bag. That was one piece of the crown collected. Three to go!

CHAPTER 4
THE GAMES MASTER

After days of trekking through the Great Ticklegrass Plains and crossing the surprisingly danger-fraught Mountains of Mildness, the two adventurers finally made it to the next spot... THE ARCANE ZONE!

The Arcane Zone was as epic as it sounded, and for lovers of games, it truly was the place to be. In every corner of this magnificent building were all manner of magical and mind-boggling

mechanisms. Some spun and chimed, some flashed with otherworldly red, blue and green lights. There were cards and joysticks and dice of all shapes and sizes. The walls were plastered with signs reading 'Win, Win, Win' and 'Level Up'. Everywhere that Ian and Waypine looked, there were games, games and more games.

There, standing in the middle of the Arcane Zone with his arms open wide, stood the Games Master. It was said throughout Fabiosa that what the Games Master lacked in strength, he more than made up for in smarts and snazzy clothes.

"Welcome, welcome!" the Games Master called to his visitors, glancing over the strange pair. "New gamers, I see." A sly grin spread across his face. "Allow me to introduce you to the Arcane Zone. Here, the rules are simple. Beat me at a game of your choice and you will be the winners of this fantastic trophy."

"I never lose. I am very good at games," Ian proclaimed, very sure of himself. Waypine wasn't quite as sure as Ian, but he translated it for the Games Master anyway. The man chuckled a bit at Ian's confidence.

"So, what will it be?" the Games Master asked, rubbing his hands together. "A deck builder? A puzzler? A role-playing game, perhaps? We have some fabulous props in the back." Ian sat down at a random table. "Aha, a strategy game. Excellent."

As the Games Master hopped onto the chair opposite the bear, Ian swiped up a piece from the board and moved it. The Games Master swung his feet happily.

"Kings. A good choice, my friend. Unfortunately for you, I am a... ahem... a master at this game," chuckled the Games Master. He reached out and plucked Ian's piece off the board.

"Hey, that's my piece," growled Ian.

"I'm afraid he is allowed to take it," said Waypine. "You see, the rules–"

"Stupid rules," interrupted the bear. "I'm just going to take the trophy."

Waypine turned to the Games Master. "My companion would like to know what is stopping him from just taking the trophy from you."

"That," said the Game Master, his grin growing thinner and wider, "would be my automatons!"

Suddenly, a small army of wooden robots from all around the Arcane Zone appeared around the table.

"I see," said Waypine. "Ian, just make the moves that I tell you to. Move that black tower forward four squares."

Ian reached for the tower, but his massive

bear paws were just not suited for this sort of thing. Every time Ian tried to pick up a piece, he knocked over four others. At each failed attempt to play the game, the bear grew angrier and angrier, until...

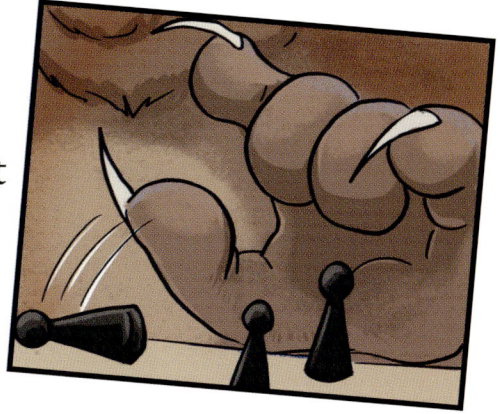

"AAAAAAAARGH!"

Ian could not put up with the silly game one minute longer. His paws may have been no good for moving small game pieces, but they were just fine at tossing large tables. In a fit of rage, Ian hurled the table into the air. Game pieces scattered everywhere. The smug smile that had been on the Game Master's face since the adventurers had arrived was suddenly replaced by an expression of pure surprise... and then by a heavy oak table! The Games Master was decidedly less smug now.

Waypine took to the air as the automatons whirred to life again. "Oh dear, oh dear, oh dear."

"BEAR-serker RAGE!" Ian roared. This was the sort of game that Ian was good at – one that involved crunching, cracking and crushing! Automatons didn't frighten him one little bit. In fact, Ian strongly felt that it had been far too long since he had last smashed something.

A wave of angry magical automatons

charged towards Ian and Waypine. One by one, and sometimes even two by two, Ian took them out with his barbarian rage. Waypine did his best to dodge the flying gears and bits of wood as the bear flung automatons left and right, into the flashing game stations and even through the roof! Soon enough, every last automaton was down.

"Good game," said Ian, brushing splinters out of his fur. Ignoring the muffled grunts of the poor Games Master stuck under the table, the bear snatched up the trophy. "Come on, Waypine. Two more to go!"

CHAPTER 5

THE PRINCESS IN PERIL

The adventurers travelled on.
They faced many hardships,
troubles and even one very
confused gnome – although
that is a story for another time.
Eventually, the heroic duo stepped
out of the enchanted Forest of Fire-
Kittens to find a tall stone tower in
the middle of nowhere.

"There it is," said Waypine.
"The third part of
the Crown of
Humanagain is
at the top of
that tower."

"I have to climb up that?" growled Ian.

"Legend has it that if you can rescue the princess at the top, she will give you her crown. Which just happens to be–"

"Gold," interrupted Ian.

"–one of the pieces we seek," Waypine finished.

As the two carried on down the path to the tower, they spied someone coming their way. The person was dressed like a prince. However, unlike most princes Waypine had run into before, he was dripping wet from head to toe.

As he passed them, the two adventurers heard the soggy prince muttering angrily. "...The cheek of it... climb the tower and rescue the princess they said... Why, I am in a mind to..."

"I guess he didn't make it to the top," Ian said.

Little did they know that the soggy prince had, in fact, made it to the top. If only they had stopped to ask the prince how exactly he had ended up dripping wet and at the bottom of the tower...

"Stay here, Ian. I will fly up to tell her to let down her hair," Waypine told the bear.

"Hair?" Ian asked, but Waypine was already too high up to hear.

Up at the tower window, Waypine spotted the

princess. Just as the legends said, her hair was as long as a dragon's tail and as bright as the golden coins piled up on her table.

"M'lady, the great adventurer Ian the Barbarian awaits you at the bottom of the tower. He has come to rescue

you," the parrot said to the princess.

"Tell him I will let my hair down for him to climb right away!" she replied, looking pleased. She had heard of Ian. Everyone had heard of Ian. He had taken a lot of gold from people, it was said. Soon, she would be the one taking all that gold from him.

The princess dangled her long locks out of the window and waited for the clueless adventurer to climb up. To her surprise, Ian was heavy. Very heavy. Much heavier than that foolish prince that she had just robbed and pushed out of the window into the icy pond below.

The princess huffed and puffed and heaved. As she pulled, she heard Ian grunting and growling. If she had been able to understand bear, she would have known that Ian was complaining about how hard it was to climb without thumbs.

Ian was finally at the top. Completely tangled in the princess's golden hair, but at the top. "I am here to rescue you, fair maiden!" he shouted. Of course, Ian being a bear, all that came out was "roar, roar, roar!"

Before Waypine could get in a word of translation, the princess let out a shriek. A huge bear was the last thing she had expected to come over that windowsill.

Quicker than a swamp goblin, the princess chopped through her own hair and dived out of the other window in a panic.

The princess's golden crown span in the air behind her after her hasty exit, then clanged and clattered to the ground. A moment later, Waypine heard a yelp and a splash from one side and a thump and a growl from the other as both the princess and the barbarian fell from the tower.

"Well, that was easy," Waypine said, swooping down to grab the crown. "Did you see all this gold, Ian?" he added, taking in the bags and bags of treasure that the scheming princess had snagged from other, less successful adventurers. "There's enough here to make a dragon jealous!"

From outside, Waypine heard the sounds of a spluttering princess and the roar of rather annoyed bear.

"Speaking of dragons..." said the wizard parrot, "To the final piece!"

CHAPTER 6

THE RIDDLE DRAGON

After an unexpectedly boring and uneventful journey over the Foothills of Ill-Fate, Ian and Waypine came to the entrance of a dark cave.

"The last piece is held by a dragon. Come on, he is inside here," said the bird.

"Am I going to get to bash a dragon?" Ian asked, excited. "I always wanted to

bash a dragon."

"No. No bashing. I don't think that would be a good idea," said Waypine. Even if Ian wasn't afraid of the thought of angering a dragon, Waypine was.

If only the wizard could have read Ian's mind right then. Ian was definitely in a dragon-bashing mood.

"Ok, no bashing," lied the bear.

Soon, the cave widened into a huge, open area. Right in the centre, sat on a massive pile of treasure, was an enormous red dragon. Somewhere in that heap of

gold and jewels was the last piece of the Crown of Humanagain.

Suddenly, a loud, rumbling voice echoed through the cave, startling Waypine so much that he let out a tiny squawk.

"Who disturbs my sleep? If it is my treasure you seek, then the answer to this riddle you must speak."

"Let me do the talking..." Waypine whispered to Ian. "Give me your riddle, dragon."

"Quiet, little bird. The riddle is for

the warrior who carries the other parts of the Crown of Humanagain," rumbled the dragon. Little wisps of smoke curled up from its snout as it spoke. "Here is your riddle: If I am meat, you should not eat. And if I am vegetable, I am consumable. What am I?"

Waypine was not very impressed by this riddle at all. He thought that dragons were supposed to be the very best of the best riddle-makers. Of course, Waypine already knew the answer, but he didn't dare say anything. Not while he was close enough to feel the fiery heat from the dragon's body! It was all on Ian now. The problem was, even if Ian could somehow solve the riddle by himself, he could still only speak in bear. Waypine was pretty sure that dragons couldn't understand bear.

Ian hummed and hawed. This riddle was really trying his bear brain. He wasn't even completely sure that he knew what the word 'consumable' meant.

"Ah ha!" said Ian. "The answer is... A STONE!" he roared confidently.

Waypine buried his face in his feathers. 'Stone' was not the right answer. Well, it looked as though he and Ian would just have to get used to being animals.

But then...

"Correct!" said the dragon. "The answer is **raw**. Take your prize and get out of my cave." The dragon fished a shiny jewel out of the treasure pile with a claw that was larger than Ian's head and gave it to the adventurers.

Waypine was amazed. Somehow, Ian's roar had sounded just like the answer to the riddle.

"I told you I was clever," Ian said, smugly.

"You mean lucky!" said the wizard.

CHAPTER 7

HUMAN AGAIN

Whether by brains or bashing or sheer bear-brained luck, Ian and Waypine now had all the pieces they needed. All they had left to do before they could undo their curse was put the parts of the Crown of Humanagain together. With Ian's clumsy paws, this was easier said than done. Still, he managed it... eventually.

"Now, simply place the crown on your head," said Waypine, watching intently from a tree branch. If he had had fingers to cross at that moment, he would have crossed them.

As soon as the bear placed the

complete crown onto his head, it started glowing with magical light. The light swirled and shifted around him. Little by little, Ian began to transform from a big, hairy bear back into a big, hairy human. He seemed very

pleased indeed to have thumbs again.

The wizard was next. Just as it had with Ian, the crown surrounded the bird in swirling wisps of light. As the magical lights faded, they revealed a tall, thin wizardy-looking fellow, complete with a wizard's bushy white beard. For the first time, Ian saw Waypine as his normal self... Well, normal but for the fact that Waypine was still perched up on a branch!

Ian helped him down from the tree. "There we go, my little friend."

Waypine wriggled his shoulders, testing out his old human muscles again. "Thank you, my friend. I have been a parrot for longer than I would like to admit. I think it's going to take a while to get used to not having wings..." Waypine took a few wobbly steps. "...And to get used to walking on these human legs again!"

"Well, you've got plenty of miles of road to practice using your legs on. We've got one last adventure to go on together," Ian said with a mischievous look in his eye.

"Oh?" said the wizard.

"Waypine, have I ever told you about the time I won a card game in the Fabled Inn? (I'm very good at games.)"

"You won? Did this card game happen to involve any bashing, by chance?" asked Waypine.

"Well, maybe a little bit," admitted Ian as they set off together down the long road to the Fabled Inn. "You see, there was this one tricksy fellow in a green hood..."

CHAPTER 8

EPILOGUE

The door to the Fabled Inn swung open.

Ian stepped through, looking as menacing and barbarian as ever.

The inn was busy, but Ian spotted the man he was looking for straight away. "There he is, Waypine," the barbarian said. "That's the hooded fool I was telling you about. He's the one that tricked me into trying to take your orb when I made him lose that card game."

"He does look a shifty fellow," said the wizard. "Have you got the sack?"

"Oh, I do," said Ian. He marched across the room, straight to the hooded figure. The man gulped nervously as he remembered what he had done to Ian all those days ago.

"Get in the sack!" Ian roared, shoving a large sack towards him.

No one in the inn dared to get in the way as the terrified man stepped into the sack. They all knew enough about Ian to know that doing that would have been a very bad idea. Ian flung the sack over his shoulder, lifting it easily even with a whole person inside. Just as suddenly as the barbarian had marched into the inn, he marched out again.

"You think you can trick me?" Ian said to the wriggling sack. "Let's see what kind of animal you are! Waypine, the orb!"

"Of course, my friend," said the wizard as he dropped the orb in, taking care to not let it touch his skin again. He had already learnt that lesson the hard way.

Magic swirled inside the sack. Before long, Ian and Waypine heard the muffled squeaks of the hooded man. Only, the hooded man was no longer a man... Out of the bag crawled a scrawny grey rat!

"I think this little adventure of ours has gone very well," said the wizard, ignoring a great deal of angry squeaking from behind him. "You know, I might just have another adventure in me."

Ian grinned. "Well, that dragon still has a lot of gold..."

The End

...for now.